WASHINGTON TEST PREP

Reading Comprehension

MSP Reading Workbook

Grade 4

ISBN 978-1477523810

CONTENTS

Introduction   4

Reading Comprehension Exercises
Reading Comprehension – Set 1   5
Reading Comprehension – Set 2   17
Reading Comprehension – Set 3   29
Reading Comprehension – Set 4   41
Reading Comprehension – Set 5   53
Reading Comprehension – Set 6   65
Reading Comprehension – Set 7   77
Reading Comprehension – Set 8   89

Answer Key   **101**
Answer Key – Set 1   102
Answer Key – Set 2   105
Answer Key – Set 3   109
Answer Key – Set 4   112
Answer Key – Set 5   115
Answer Key – Set 6   118
Answer Key – Set 7   121
Answer Key – Set 8   123

Score Tracker   **125**

INTRODUCTION
For Parents, Teachers, and Tutors

About the Book

The MSP Reading test taken by all Washington students contains reading passages followed by reading comprehension questions. The reading comprehension questions assess the skills described in the Common Core Standards for English Language Arts. This workbook will develop the skills that students need for the state test, while also preparing students for the types of questions they will answer on the state test.

Ongoing Reading Comprehension Practice

This workbook allows students to have ongoing test prep practice as part of their homework routine. Without the stress of long complex passages and long question sets, students can develop the reading skills needed while gaining confidence and becoming familiar with answering reading comprehension questions.

Developing Common Core Skills

The state of Washington has adopted the Common Core standards. These standards describe what students are expected to know. Student learning is based on these standards throughout the year, and the state test includes questions that assess whether students have the skills described in the standards.

The skills described in the Common Core standards cover reading, writing, and language. Each passage in this workbook includes a Core Skills Practice exercise. Each exercise focuses on one key reading, writing, or language skill. By completing these exercises, students will develop the core skills that grade 4 students are expected to have.

Preparing for the MSP Reading Test

This reading comprehension workbook contains passages and question sets similar to those on the MSP Reading test, but much shorter. The multiple-choice questions are just like those found on the MSP test and cover all the same skills. The Core Skills Practice exercises included with each passage will develop the core skills that students will need to perform well on the state test. The last passage in each set also has an extended-response question. This question will give students practice providing written answers and will ensure that students can understand, analyze, and respond to passages.

Reading Comprehension

MSP Reading

Set 1

Instructions

Read each passage. Complete the exercise under each passage.

Then complete the questions on the next page. For each multiple-choice question, read the question carefully. Then select the best answer. Fill in the circle for the correct answer.

The Basement Door

Jake had always been scared of the basement. Its heavy wooden door made a long slow creaking sound that sent shivers down his spine. His parents had always warned him not to go down there.

One day, Jake pushed the door open and began to tiptoe down the wooden stairs. As he reached the middle step, he heard a loud bang from deep inside the basement's darkness. He turned sharply and hurried back up the stairs. He never tried to go down into the basement again.

CORE SKILLS PRACTICE

Imagine that Jake decides to face his fear again. This time, he does go all the way down into the basement. Write a short story about how Jake overcomes his fear.

_____

_____

_____

_____

_____

_____

_____

_____

1   Why does Jake leave the basement?

    Ⓐ   His parents tell him to.

    Ⓑ   The door creaks.

    Ⓒ   He hears a loud noise.

    Ⓓ   He sees something scary.

2   What is the first paragraph mostly about?

    Ⓐ   What the basement door sounds like

    Ⓑ   What happens when Jake goes into the basement

    Ⓒ   Why Jake decides to go down into the basement

    Ⓓ   How Jake feels about the basement

3   Read this sentence from the passage.

He turned sharply and hurried back up the stairs.

What does the word <u>sharply</u> show about Jake?

    Ⓐ   He tripped over.

    Ⓑ   He turned slowly.

    Ⓒ   He turned suddenly.

    Ⓓ   He hurt himself.

The Rubik's Cube

The Rubik's Cube is a three dimensional mechanical puzzle. It was designed and created by Hungarian sculptor Erno Rubik. Erno Rubik probably had no idea how popular it would become.

It was first invented in 1974. It has six faces covered by nine stickers of different color. The challenge is to spin and move the cube until all sides are covered by a single color. This sounds like a simple puzzle to solve. But it is actually quite difficult.

The cube was licensed to be sold by Ideal Toy Corp in 1980. It has since become one of the world's most successful toys. It has sold over 350 million units.

CORE SKILLS PRACTICE

The passage uses several proper nouns. Proper nouns name a certain person, place, thing, or idea. Complete the table by listing the four proper nouns from the passage next to its correct type.

Type of Proper Noun	Example of Proper Noun
item	
nationality	
person's name	
company name	

1   Which two words from the passage have about the same meaning?

    Ⓐ   *created, invented*

    Ⓑ   *licensed, sold*

    Ⓒ   *simple, difficult*

    Ⓓ   *challenge, popular*

2   Which sentence from the passage best supports the idea that the Rubik's Cube is popular?

    Ⓐ   *The Rubik's Cube is a three dimensional mechanical puzzle.*

    Ⓑ   *It was designed and created by Hungarian sculptor Erno Rubik.*

    Ⓒ   *The challenge is to spin and move the cube until all sides are covered by a single color.*

    Ⓓ   *It has sold over 350 million units.*

3   Which detail about the Rubik's Cube is an opinion?

    Ⓐ   It was first invented in 1974.

    Ⓑ   It has six faces.

    Ⓒ   It is difficult to solve.

    Ⓓ   It was designed by a sculptor.

Learning Lines

Thomas had been practicing his lines for the play since breakfast. No matter how hard he tried, he just could not remember his opening words. He had only stopped for lunch and dinner. Even then, he had wolfed down his food and gotten right back to work. He was beginning to feel like he would never get them right. Finally, as it began to get dark, he managed to complete his entire speech without using his script.

"Ha!" he said. "I knew that if I kept trying I would be able to remember the words!"

CORE SKILLS PRACTICE

The theme of a story is the message of a story, or what you can learn from the story. What is the theme or message of the story? Describe how you could use the message of the story in your own life.

_____

_____

_____

_____

_____

_____

_____

1   Read this sentence from the passage.

    **Even then, he had wolfed down his food and gotten right back to
    work.**

    Why does the author use the word <u>wolfed</u> in the sentence?

    Ⓐ   To show that Thomas talked while eating

    Ⓑ   To show that Thomas ate a large meal

    Ⓒ   To show that Thomas ate quickly

    Ⓓ   To show that Thomas enjoyed his food

2   How does Thomas most likely feel at the end of the passage?

    Ⓐ   Stressed

    Ⓑ   Upset

    Ⓒ   Proud

    Ⓓ   Silly

3   What is the main theme of the passage?

    Ⓐ   Hard work will pay off.

    Ⓑ   Plays are a lot of work.

    Ⓒ   A good memory is helpful.

    Ⓓ   Learn when to quit.

Sir Isaac Newton

Sir Isaac Newton is one of the most important scientists ever. He made many important achievements. He studied math and physics. In today's society, he is best known for his discovery of gravity.

Isaac Newton also developed laws of motion, or laws that explain how things move. It is a little known fact that he also built one of the first telescopes. Newton developed many theories about mathematics and physics that are still used today.

CORE SKILLS PRACTICE

The author gives brief information about Isaac Newton. Imagine you want to write a more detailed report about Isaac Newton. What else would you want to include in the report? Write a list of questions you could research and answer in your report.

1. _____

2. _____

3. _____

4. _____

5. _____

6. _____

1 Read this sentence from the passage.

> **Newton developed many theories about mathematics and physics that are still used today.**

Which meaning of the word <u>developed</u> is used in the sentence?

Ⓐ   Grew older

Ⓑ   Became larger

Ⓒ   Created

Ⓓ   Ripened

2 How is the passage mainly organized?

Ⓐ   A solution to a problem is described.

Ⓑ   Events are described in the order they occurred.

Ⓒ   Facts are given to support an argument.

Ⓓ   An event in the past is compared to an event today.

3 Which of the following was NOT an achievement of Newton's?

Ⓐ   Building a telescope

Ⓑ   Discovering gravity

Ⓒ   Developing laws of motion

Ⓓ   Creating models of atoms

In the End

Michael heard the starting pistol and began to run as fast as he could. As he pulled ahead of Stephen, he felt confident that he would win the race. Michael kept running as fast as he could. He started to get a nice lead. Stephen ran at a steady pace, taking care not to wear himself out.

As they both reached the final straight, Michael began to tire. He had been running so hard that he had no energy left. He began to slow. Stephen maintained his own pace and overtook Michael with his final stride. The race and the gold medal were won by Stephen.

CORE SKILLS PRACTICE

Sometimes you will be asked to compare or contrast two characters. This means that you decide what is similar about the two characters or what is different about the two characters. Contrast Michael and Stephen by answering the question below.

How is Michael's approach to the race different from Stephen's?

_____

_____

_____

_____

_____

_____

---

1   Read this sentence from the passage.

> **Stephen maintained his own pace and overtook Michael with his final stride.**

As it is used in the sentence, what does <u>maintained</u> mean?

Ⓐ   Increased slightly

Ⓑ   Kept steady

Ⓒ   Looked after

Ⓓ   Improved upon

2   Which statement best describes the theme of the passage?

Ⓐ   Slow and steady wins the race.

Ⓑ   It is better to be safe than sorry.

Ⓒ   There is only one winner.

Ⓓ   Life is full of surprises.

3   How is the passage mainly organized?

Ⓐ   A solution to a problem is described.

Ⓑ   Events are described in the order they occurred.

Ⓒ   Facts are given to support an argument.

Ⓓ   An event in the past is compared to an event today.

4 How does Stephen most likely feel after the race? Use information from the passage to support your answer.

DIRECTIONS Be sure to:
- Write your answer in your own words.
- Write clearly.
- Check your answer after writing it.

_____

_____

_____

_____

_____

_____

_____

_____

_____

Reading Comprehension

MSP Reading

Set 2

Instructions

Read each passage. Complete the exercise under each passage.

Then complete the questions on the next page. For each multiple-choice question, read the question carefully. Then select the best answer. Fill in the circle for the correct answer.

Sarah's Diary

Ever since she had been a little girl, Sarah had always written her thoughts in a diary. Although she felt comfortable talking to her sister and parents, she liked to record the details of her day. Sarah found it comforting and it helped her to relax at the end of a long day. Sometimes, when Sarah was alone, she would look back at days where she was sad and think about just how far she had come.

Sarah's mother thought it was a good way to spend an hour each afternoon. Sarah's sister often wondered what Sarah was writing about. But she knew it was important not to read her sister's diary.

CORE SKILLS PRACTICE

The passage describes how Sarah finds writing in her diary relaxing. It also describes how she feels good when she looks back at sad times. What other benefits do you think writing in a diary could have?

_____

_____

_____

_____

_____

---

1   Read this sentence from the passage.

> **Sarah found it comforting and it helped her to relax at the end of a long day.**

What does the word <u>comforting</u> mean?

Ⓐ   Calming

Ⓑ   Challenging

Ⓒ   Upsetting

Ⓓ   Exciting

2   Based on the information in the passage, which word best describes Sarah?

Ⓐ   Outgoing

Ⓑ   Shy

Ⓒ   Caring

Ⓓ   Thoughtful

3   What is the point of view in the passage?

Ⓐ   First person

Ⓑ   Second person

Ⓒ   Third person limited

Ⓓ   Third person omniscient

Soccer

Soccer is a ball sport that was invented in England in the 1800s. It is an outdoor sport. An individual match sees two teams of 11 players compete against each other. The object of the game is to work the ball into one of the two goals positioned at each end of the field.

It is a sport that is played all over the world. It is very popular in South America and Europe. The most successful international team is Brazil. They have won five World Cups since 1930, which is a competition that is held every 4 years. Italy has won four World Cups. Germany is not far behind, with three wins.

Soccer is not as popular as sports like baseball and basketball in the United States. However, it is a very entertaining sport to watch. Soccer may become a favorite sport in the United States one day.

CORE SKILLS PRACTICE

To understand information, it can help to put it in order. Complete the table below by adding information about the three most successful international teams. Place the teams in order from most successful to least successful.

Most Successful International Teams	Number of World Cup Wins Since 1930
1.	
2.	
3.	

1   Read this sentence from the passage.

> **The object of the game is to work the ball into one of the two goals positioned at each end of the field.**

Which meaning of the word <u>object</u> is used in the sentence above?

Ⓐ   A goal or aim

Ⓑ   A type of item

Ⓒ   To argue against

Ⓓ   To refuse to do something

2   Which detail from the passage is an opinion?

Ⓐ   Soccer was invented in the 1800s.

Ⓑ   Soccer is an outdoor sport.

Ⓒ   Soccer teams have 11 players each.

Ⓓ   Soccer is entertaining to watch.

3   Where was the game of soccer invented?

Ⓐ   England

Ⓑ   Brazil

Ⓒ   Italy

Ⓓ   Germany

Pompeii

Ancient Pompeii is a partially buried Roman city in southern Italy. It was destroyed and completely buried after the eruption of Mount Vesuvius in 79AD. Despite being buried by over 4 meters of ash, the city was rediscovered in 1599. It has since been excavated and preserved. It is now one of the most popular tourist attractions in Italy. The city is referred to as Ancient Pompeii as a modern city of Pompeii exists in Naples.

Notes
Excavated – to remove soil or earth by digging
Preserved – to keep from spoiling

©Wikimedia Commons

CORE SKILLS PRACTICE

You can often work out what a word means by how it is used in a passage. Locate the words below in the passage. Write a definition of each word.

partially: _____

destroyed: _____

popular: _____

---

1   Read this sentence from the passage.

Despite being buried by over 4 meters of ash, the city was rediscovered in 1599.

What does the word <u>rediscovered</u> mean?

Ⓐ   Discovered before

Ⓑ   Discovered again

Ⓒ   Not discovered

Ⓓ   Less discovered

2   What is the main purpose of the notes at the end of the passage?

Ⓐ   To list important details about Pompeii

Ⓑ   To describe how Ancient Pompeii was found

Ⓒ   To give the meaning of difficult words

Ⓓ   To indicate the sources the author used

3   The passage was probably written mainly to –

Ⓐ   teach people about an ancient site

Ⓑ   persuade readers to visit Italy

Ⓒ   tell an entertaining story

Ⓓ   inform readers about volcanoes

The Bumble Bee

Yellow and black with a set of tiny wings,
I busily buzz around the land,
And boast a mighty sting!

I do not care for fame or money,
I do not wish to harm,
I just live for making honey!

CORE SKILLS PRACTICE

This short poem is about a bumble bee. Select an animal of your choice. Write a short poem about that animal. You may choose to have your poem rhyme like this one does, or you may write a poem that does not rhyme.

1 According to the poem, what does the bee enjoy most?

   Ⓐ   Being famous

   Ⓑ   Being rich

   Ⓒ   Making honey

   Ⓓ   Stinging people

2 Read this line from the poem.

I busily buzz around the land,

Which literary device is used in this line?

   Ⓐ   Alliteration

   Ⓑ   Simile

   Ⓒ   Metaphor

   Ⓓ   Imagery

3 What is the rhyme pattern of each stanza of the poem?

   Ⓐ   Every line rhymes.

   Ⓑ   The first and second lines rhyme.

   Ⓒ   The first and last lines rhyme.

   Ⓓ   None of the lines rhyme.

Crying Wolf

Jack had a naughty side. He sometimes liked to pretend that he was sick so he could have the day off school. He did this several times, but his parents began to realize what he was up to.

One day Jack really was feeling unwell, and so he told his parents the moment he woke up. They thought he was being naughty though, and sent him to school anyway. Jack felt ill all day, and he never pretended to be ill again.

CORE SKILLS PRACTICE

The first sentence of the passage states that Jack is naughty. How does the author show that Jack is naughty?

_____

_____

_____

_____

_____

_____

_____

1   What will Jack most likely do the next time he does not want to go to school?

    Ⓐ   Tell his parents that he is ill

    Ⓑ   Accept that he has to go to school

    Ⓒ   Make up a better excuse for not going

    Ⓓ   Tell his teacher that he feels unwell

2   Why do Jack's parents send him to school when he says that he is ill?

    Ⓐ   They think that school is too important.

    Ⓑ   They want to teach him a lesson.

    Ⓒ   They do not believe that he is ill.

    Ⓓ   They believe that he will get getter soon.

3   What lesson does Jack learn in the passage?

    Ⓐ   Look after yourself.

    Ⓑ   Listen to your parents.

    Ⓒ   Always be truthful.

    Ⓓ   Small lies are not harmful.

4 What is the main lesson that readers can learn from the passage? Use information from the passage to support your answer.

DIRECTIONS Be sure to:
- Write your answer in your own words.
- Write clearly.
- Check your answer after writing it.

_____

_____

_____

_____

_____

_____

_____

_____

_____

Reading Comprehension

MSP Reading

Set 3

Instructions

Read each passage. Complete the exercise under each passage.

Then complete the questions on the next page. For each multiple-choice question, read the question carefully. Then select the best answer. Fill in the circle for the correct answer.

Big Ben

Big Ben is one of the United Kingdom's most famous landmarks. It is located in the Palace of Westminster in London. Big Ben is the term given to refer to the great bell of the clock at the north end of the building. Over time, the nickname has been used to refer to the clock and the clock tower too.

Its building was completed in April 1858, and it celebrated its 150th anniversary in 2009. Even though it is over 150 years old, it still looks pretty. It is the third largest free standing clock in the world.

CORE SKILLS PRACTICE

Locate the information in the passage to answer the questions below.

In what country is Big Ben located?

_____

In what building is Big Ben located?

_____

When was Big Ben built?

_____

What was celebrated in 2009?

_____

---

1   Read this sentence from the passage.

Even though it is over 150 years old, it still looks pretty.

Which word means the opposite of <u>pretty</u>?

Ⓐ   Lovely

Ⓑ   Ugly

Ⓒ   Old

Ⓓ   Modern

2   What is the main purpose of the passage?

Ⓐ   To inform readers about a famous clock

Ⓑ   To persuade readers to visit Big Ben

Ⓒ   To compare Big Ben to other clocks

Ⓓ   To teach readers how to find the clock

3   Which sentence from the passage contains an opinion?

Ⓐ   *It is located in the Palace of Westminster in London.*

Ⓑ   *Its building was completed in April 1858, and it celebrated its 150th anniversary in 2009.*

Ⓒ   *Even though it is over 150 years old, it still looks pretty.*

Ⓓ   *It is the third largest free standing clock in the world.*

Alexander Graham Bell

Alexander Graham Bell is a famous inventor. He was born in Scotland in 1847. He is best known for inventing the telephone. His achievement was based on his research into hearing and speech. He was awarded a US patent for his invention in 1876. His telephone was quite different to those of today.

The following years saw his creation become used worldwide. Bell disliked the attention that his invention brought to him. Even though he invented it, he disliked telephones. He preferred to be left alone and not bothered. He did not even have a telephone in his place of work. He died in August, 1922.

Poor Elisha Gray

At the same time that Bell was developing his telephone, an inventor named Elisha Gray was developing his. Gray applied for a patent on his invention on the same day as Bell. However, Gray applied several hours after Bell. Alexander Graham Bell was awarded the patent for the first telephone. If Elisha Gray had been just a few hours quicker, he would be much more well known today.

CORE SKILLS PRACTICE

How do you think Elisha Gray would have felt when Alexander Graham Bell was awarded the patent for the first telephone?

_____

_____

_____

_____

1   Which detail about Alexander Graham Bell would be least important to include in a summary of his life?

  Ⓐ   He was born in Scotland in 1847.

  Ⓑ   He is best known for inventing the telephone.

  Ⓒ   He was awarded a patent for the telephone in 1876.

  Ⓓ   He did not have a telephone in his place of work.

2   What type of passage is "Alexander Graham Bell"?

  Ⓐ   Biography

  Ⓑ   Autobiography

  Ⓒ   Diary

  Ⓓ   News article

3   How is the information in the passage mainly organized?

  Ⓐ   A problem is described and then a solution is given.

  Ⓑ   Events are described in the order they occurred.

  Ⓒ   An argument is made and then facts are given.

  Ⓓ   The first telephone is compared to telephones today.

Penny the Princess

Penny was a beautiful princess. She lived in a tall towering castle that almost reached the clouds. What people didn't know was that she had special super wishing powers. But Penny often failed to use them because she had everything she had ever wanted. She had no need to wish for food, or pretty things, or happy times. Every day was pleasant for Penny.

One day, a homeless man visited her and asked for help. Penny used her powers to give him money, a cozy home, and fresh food. Penny was shocked by how pleased the man was. She had never realized how lucky she was. From that day forward, she decided to use her powers to help as many people as she could.

CORE SKILLS PRACTICE

Many stories involve cause and effect. The cause is the reason for something. The effect is what happens. Answer the question about cause and effect.

What effect does meeting the homeless man have on Penny?

_____

_____

_____

_____

_____

---

1   Read this sentence from the passage.

She lived in a tall towering castle that almost reached the clouds.

Which literary device is used in the sentence?

ⓐ   Simile, comparing the castle to a cloud

ⓑ   Imagery, using words to create a picture of the castle

ⓒ   Metaphor, showing that the castle is like a cloud

ⓓ   Hyperbole, overstating how tall the castle is

2   How does Penny change in the passage?

ⓐ   She realizes how much she can help others.

ⓑ   She realizes that she has everything she needs.

ⓒ   She realizes that she has special wishing powers.

ⓓ   She realizes that she has used her wishes too often.

3   Which term best describes the passage?

ⓐ   Historical fiction

ⓑ   Science fiction

ⓒ   Autobiography

ⓓ   Fable

Making Mistakes

Kelly was trying to do her homework. She kept making mistakes with her division. Each time she tried, it was still wrong. Her father was doing his best to help her.

"It's alright Kelly," he said. "Everybody makes mistakes."

Her father's calmness helped to calm Kelly down too. He also reminded her that getting upset wouldn't help. She took a deep breath and continued to work. She finally managed to complete all of her questions.

"Thanks Dad," she said. "I guess it is all right to make mistakes as long as you fix them."

CORE SKILLS PRACTICE

A summary is a description of the events of a story. A summary should include only the main events from the story. Write a summary of the story "Making Mistakes."

_____

_____

_____

_____

_____

1   What is the main lesson that is learned in the passage?

   Ⓐ   It is important not to give up.

   Ⓑ   Math can sometimes be hard.

   Ⓒ   Parents should help their children.

   Ⓓ   It is easy to get angry at yourself.

2   How does Kelly most likely feel in the first paragraph?

   Ⓐ   Proud

   Ⓑ   Calm

   Ⓒ   Tired

   Ⓓ   Upset

3   Which word best describes Kelly's father?

   Ⓐ   Cranky

   Ⓑ   Helpful

   Ⓒ   Fun

   Ⓓ   Lazy

Mount Mauna Kea

It is well known that Mount Everest is the world's highest mountain above sea level. But what about mountains that start beneath the water's surface? If we look at these, then Mount Mauna Kea is the tallest anywhere in the world.

Mount Mauna Kea is an inactive volcano on the island of Hawaii. It is more than 6 miles tall from the seabed to its summit. This makes Mount Mauna Kea almost 1 mile taller than Mount Everest.

©Vadim Kurland

CORE SKILLS PRACTICE

Imagine you want to add a diagram to make it easier to compare Mount Mauna Kea and Mount Everest. Describe what the diagram would look like.

_____

_____

_____

_____

_____

1   Which word means the opposite of <u>beneath</u>?

    Ⓐ   Above

    Ⓑ   Under

    Ⓒ   Near

    Ⓓ   Along

2   Which sentence from the passage best summarizes the main idea?

    Ⓐ   *It is well known that Mount Everest is the world's highest mountain above sea level.*

    Ⓑ   *Mount Mauna Kea is an inactive volcano on the island of Hawaii.*

    Ⓒ   *It is more than 6 miles tall from the seabed to its summit.*

    Ⓓ   *This makes Mount Mauna Kea almost 1 mile taller than Mount Everest.*

3   If the passage were given another title, which title would best fit?

    Ⓐ   All About Mount Everest

    Ⓑ   The Real World's Tallest Mountain

    Ⓒ   How Mountains Form

    Ⓓ   The Dangers of Volcanoes

4   Explain how Mount Everest and Mount Mauna Kea are similar. Explain how Mount Everest and Mount Mauna Kea are different. Use information from the passage to support your answer.

DIRECTIONS Be sure to:

         - Write your answer in your own words.

         - Write clearly.

         - Check your answer after writing it.

_____

_____

_____

_____

_____

_____

_____

_____

Reading Comprehension

MSP Reading

Set 4

Instructions

Read each passage. Complete the exercise under each passage.

Then complete the questions on the next page. For each multiple-choice question, read the question carefully. Then select the best answer. Fill in the circle for the correct answer.

The First World War

The First World War was fought between 1914 and 1918. It was fought with Austria, Hungary, and Germany on one side. These countries were known as the Central Powers. England, France, and Russia were on the other side. These countries were known as the Allies. The United States joined the conflict in 1917. The United States joined the Allies. The German forces agreed to a ceasefire in November of that year.

First World War begins		The United States enters the war	First World War ends
July, 1914		April, 1917	November, 1918

CORE SKILLS PRACTICE	
Summarize the information in the passage by completing the table below with the names of the countries that made up each group.	
The Central Powers	**The Allies**

1   What does the timeline best show?

Ⓐ   What caused the First World War

Ⓑ   When the events of the war occurred

Ⓒ   Why the United States entered the war

Ⓓ   Where the main events of the war occurred

2   Where would this passage most likely be found?

Ⓐ   In an encyclopedia

Ⓑ   In an atlas

Ⓒ   In a travel guide

Ⓓ   In a book of short stories

3   What is the main purpose of the passage?

Ⓐ   To instruct

Ⓑ   To entertain

Ⓒ   To persuade

Ⓓ   To inform

Football

Molly loved football. Whenever the boys played on the field, she always joined in and gave it her all. Her older brothers all played football. Ever since she was young, she had joined in with them when they played in the park.

One day the coach had to choose a team to play against another local school. He had watched Molly play often. He decided to pick her. Molly could hardly believe it. She had not expected to be picked at all. She would be the only girl on the team. Her brothers were surprised too. But they were happy for her.

CORE SKILLS PRACTICE

The title of this passage is "Football." A better title for the passage would describe what the passage is about. Think of a new title for the passage. Write the title below, and then explain why it would be a good title for the passage.

Title: _____

_____

_____

_____

_____

_____

---

1   Read this sentence from the passage.

> **Whenever the boys played on the field, she always joined in and gave it her all.**

What does the phrase "gave it her all" show about Molly?

Ⓐ   She gave the boys a gift.

Ⓑ   She was not good at football.

Ⓒ   She tried very hard.

Ⓓ   She scored many points.

2   What is the most likely reason Molly did not expect to be picked?

Ⓐ   She is female.

Ⓑ   She does not know how to play.

Ⓒ   She is not old enough.

Ⓓ   She loves playing football.

3   How does Molly most likely feel about being picked for the team?

Ⓐ   Shocked and scared

Ⓑ   Surprised, but happy

Ⓒ   Confused and annoyed

Ⓓ   Excited, but worried

The Olympics

The Olympics are a global sporting event. They feature both outdoor and indoor sports. They are watched and enjoyed by people all over the world. They are an important event because they bring people from all countries together.

They are held in both a summer and winter format. The Winter Olympics and Summer Olympics are both held every 4 years. The first modern Olympics were held in 1896. Many nations compete in each Olympic event. A different country hosts the games each time. The city of London in the United Kingdom is the host of the 2012 Olympics.

Year	Held
2012	London, United Kingdom
2008	Beijing, China
2004	Athens, Greece
2000	Sydney, Australia
1996	Atlanta, United States
1992	Barcelona, Spain

CORE SKILLS PRACTICE

It can take years of training to win an Olympic medal. People often have to give up a lot to even compete in the Olympics. Do you think winning an Olympic medal is a worthwhile goal? Explain your answer.

_____

_____

_____

_____

_____

1 Which sentence from the passage is an opinion?

Ⓐ *They are an important event because they bring people from all countries together.*

Ⓑ *The Winter Olympics and Summer Olympics are both held every 4 years.*

Ⓒ The first modern Olympics were held in 1896.

Ⓓ *The city of London in the United Kingdom is the host of the 2012 Olympics.*

2 Which word means about the same as <u>global</u>?

Ⓐ Athletic

Ⓑ Worldwide

Ⓒ Popular

Ⓓ Recent

3 According to the table, in which year were the Olympic Games held in America?

Ⓐ 2008

Ⓑ 2004

Ⓒ 2000

Ⓓ 1996

Air

You may think of oxygen as the main gas in air, but it is actually nitrogen. Nitrogen accounts for 78 percent of the air that we breathe. Only 21 percent of the air is made up of oxygen.

The high amount of nitrogen in the air is the result of volcanic eruptions during the Earth's early history. Less than 1 percent of air is made up of carbon dioxide. Argon is the only other major gas in air. It accounts for less than 1 percent of its makeup.

CORE SKILLS PRACTICE

Many passages include photographs. These support the information in the passage. Describe what the photograph helps the reader understand.

_____

_____

_____

_____

---

1   How is the first paragraph organized?

Ⓐ   A problem is described and then a solution is given.

Ⓑ   Events are described in the order they occurred.

Ⓒ   A statement is made and then facts are given to support it.

Ⓓ   A cause is described and then its effect is shown.

2   What is the main gas in the air?

Ⓐ   Oxygen

Ⓑ   Nitrogen

Ⓒ   Carbon dioxide

Ⓓ   Argon

3   Which of the following would be best to add to the passage to support the information?

Ⓐ   A timeline of the major events in the Earth's history

Ⓑ   A graph showing how much of each gas makes up the atmosphere

Ⓒ   A photograph showing what the atmosphere looks like

Ⓓ   A table describing the atmospheres of different planets

The Waggiest Tail

Melanie and Becky both had puppies. They took them to the park together twice a week. The puppies would play and chase each other. Melanie would often say that her dog had the waggiest tail.

"My dog has a waggier tail than yours," said Melanie, as they walked home one day.

"Oh, no she doesn't," said Becky.

Melanie and Becky argued about it the rest of the way home. When they got home, they asked Melanie's mother which dog had the waggiest tail. Melanie's mother watched the dogs closely for a few minutes.

"They both have very waggy tails," she said. "So they are both happy dogs. Isn't that the most important thing?"

CORE SKILLS PRACTICE

The words "waggier" and "waggiest" are not really words, but the author uses them anyway. Why do you think the author uses these words?

_____

_____

_____

_____

_____

_____

1   Which statement best explains how you can tell that the passage is realistic fiction?

Ⓐ   The events take place outdoors.

Ⓑ   The events described could really happen.

Ⓒ   The passage has a girl as the main character.

Ⓓ   The passage contains facts and opinions.

2   Which statement best describes what the passage is about?

Ⓐ   Two girls with unhappy dogs

Ⓑ   Two girls that fight about everything

Ⓒ   Two girls that argue about something silly

Ⓓ   Two girls that like playing in the park

3   Based on the passage, what does a wagging tail show about a dog?

Ⓐ   It is fit.

Ⓑ   It is hungry.

Ⓒ   It is happy.

Ⓓ   It is thirsty.

4 What does the author want the reader to learn from Melanie and Becky? Use information from the passage to support your answer.

DIRECTIONS Be sure to:
- Write your answer in your own words.
- Write clearly.
- Check your answer after writing it.

_____

_____

_____

_____

_____

_____

_____

_____

Reading Comprehension

MSP Reading

Set 5

Instructions

Read each passage. Complete the exercise under each passage.

Then complete the questions on the next page. For each multiple-choice question, read the question carefully. Then select the best answer. Fill in the circle for the correct answer.

Beneath the Stars

Brian loved camping. He liked to take his family every summer. They would drive up near the lake and find a peaceful spot far from everything. They would pitch their tents on the first day and spend the night beneath the stars.

Alice, his younger daughter, was a little scared of the dark. She needed to be cuddled before she went to sleep. As they sat in the moonlight, Brian sang her a lullaby as he held her in his arms. She slowly drifted off to sleep and enjoyed the most wonderful dreams.

CORE SKILLS PRACTICE

The story describes something that Brian likes doing. Write about something that you enjoy doing. Be sure to include details to show what you like about it.

_____

_____

_____

_____

_____

_____

_____

1   Which words in the passage create a feeling of calm?

     Ⓐ   *every summer*

     Ⓑ   *pitch their tents*

     Ⓒ   *a little scared*

     Ⓓ   *slowly drifted off*

2   Which word would Brian most likely use to describe the camping trips?

     Ⓐ   Exciting

     Ⓑ   Stressful

     Ⓒ   Scary

     Ⓓ   Relaxing

3   What is the point of view in the passage?

     Ⓐ   First person

     Ⓑ   Second person

     Ⓒ   Third person limited

     Ⓓ   Third person omniscient

Dearest Donna

One year together, one year of bliss,
You brighten my days with your tender kiss.
I hope that you'll be my sweet valentine,
And say that you will always be mine.

In the future we may well get married,
On the wings of love we'll be carried.
As we grow old as one and together,
Side by side as partners for ever.

CORE SKILLS PRACTICE

Poets sometimes write poems for a certain audience. This poem has an audience of just one person. Explain who the poem was written for and why the poet wrote the poem.

_____

_____

_____

_____

_____

---

1   What is the tone of the poem?

Ⓐ   Sad

Ⓑ   Cheerful

Ⓒ   Playful

Ⓓ   Loving

2   What is the rhyme pattern of each stanza of the poem?

Ⓐ   Every line rhymes.

Ⓑ   The second and fourth lines rhyme.

Ⓒ   The first and last lines rhyme.

Ⓓ   There are two sets of rhyming lines.

3   Read this line from the poem.

One year together, one year of bliss,

What does the word <u>bliss</u> mean?

Ⓐ   Being alone

Ⓑ   Being married

Ⓒ   Great happiness

Ⓓ   A feeling of concern

Mozart

Mozart is a famous German composer of the classical era. He is also known as Wolfgang Amadeus Mozart. He has composed over 600 pieces of classical music. These include works for the piano and violin, as well as whole operas.

Mozart began composing at the age of 5. At this time, he wrote small pieces for his father. He continued to learn and write music all through his youth. When he was 17, he worked as a court musician in Austria. He was given the opportunity to write a range of musical pieces. Mozart left Austria in search of better work, and lived in Paris for over a year. During this time, he was unable to find work, but he still continued writing music. He then moved to Vienna. Mozart wrote most of his best-known work while living in Vienna. He died at the age of 35 in 1791.

CORE SKILLS PRACTICE

The passage describes how Mozart lived in several different countries. Write a summary of the countries Mozart lived in and what he did in each place.

_____

_____

_____

_____

_____

_____

1   Read this sentence from the passage.

He has composed over 600 pieces of classical music.

What does the word <u>composed</u> most likely refer to?

Ⓐ   Playing a song

Ⓑ   Writing a song

Ⓒ   Singing a song

Ⓓ   Listening to a song

2   What type of passage is "Mozart"?

Ⓐ   Realistic fiction

Ⓑ   Biography

Ⓒ   Autobiography

Ⓓ   Fable

3   If the passage were given another title, which title would best fit?

Ⓐ   The Life of a Great Composer

Ⓑ   How to Compose Music

Ⓒ   Living in Austria

Ⓓ   Learn the Piano Today

Raindrops

It is a popular belief that rain falls in droplets shaped like teardrops. Raindrops are often drawn to look this way. If you've ever watched a weather report on the news, you might have seen symbols representing rainfall. The raindrops are often shown as if they are teardrops. This is a nice idea, but not a practical one.

Raindrops are actually spherical rather than teardrop-shaped. This is a common property of falling liquid. Raindrops also change shape depending on how they are falling. If they are falling fast, the bottom might be pushed up. The top will then stay rounded, but the bottom will be pushed flat. The shape is a little like the top of a mushroom.

CORE SKILLS PRACTICE		
Complete the table below by drawing a shape in each box.		
How People Think Raindrops are Shaped	What Most Raindrops are Shaped Like	What Raindrops that are Falling Fast Look Like

1   Read this sentence from the passage.

Raindrops are spherical rather than teardrop-shaped.

The word <u>spherical</u> comes from the word *sphere.* What does the word <u>spherical</u> most likely mean?

Ⓐ   Clear

Ⓑ   Oval

Ⓒ   Rounded

Ⓓ   Shiny

2   If the author added another sentence to the end of the passage, what would it most likely describe?

Ⓐ   How to predict rain

Ⓑ   How ball bearings are made

Ⓒ   What other items are round

Ⓓ   Other ideas people have about rain

3   What is the first paragraph mostly about?

Ⓐ   What raindrops are actually shaped like

Ⓑ   Why raindrops are not oval

Ⓒ   How people think raindrops are shaped

Ⓓ   How to see what raindrops looks like

Visiting the Circus

Mickey didn't like clowns. When his family told him that he would be going to the circus, he was excited. He knew there would be lions, camels, and a trapeze artist. Then he remembered that there would also be clowns. He became very nervous.

"Don't worry," said his father. "You'll be fine. Your mother and I will be with you."

Mickey felt a little better and decided to go. He took his seat in the front row of the audience. As the clowns came out onto the stage, Mickey froze. Mickey's father took hold of his hand and squeezed it gently. Mickey thought about running off, even though he wasn't really sure what he was afraid of. But he sat quietly in his seat reminding himself over and over that there was nothing to fear. His hands shook a little, but he managed to stay quite calm. Gradually, his feelings of fear faded away. He started to smile as the clowns pranced around. By the time the performance was over, Mickey was giggling along with everyone else in the audience.

CORE SKILLS PRACTICE

You can tell a lot about characters by what they do. Think about what Mickey does in the story. How can you tell that Mickey is afraid?

_____

_____

_____

_____

_____

_____

1   Read this sentence from the passage.

Mickey's father took hold of his hand and squeezed it gently.

What does the word <u>gently</u> mean in the sentence above?

Ⓐ   Firmly

Ⓑ   Quietly

Ⓒ   Softly

Ⓓ   Kindly

2   What is Mickey's main problem in the passage?

Ⓐ   He is afraid of seeing the clowns.

Ⓑ   He does not want to see the lions.

Ⓒ   He wants to go to the circus with his friends.

Ⓓ   He does not understand that clowns are funny.

3   The author says that "Mickey froze" when the clowns came out onto the stage. Why does the author say this?

Ⓐ   To show that Mickey was surprised

Ⓑ   To emphasize how scared Mickey felt

Ⓒ   To explain why Mickey was afraid

Ⓓ   To suggest that Mickey was acting

4   What details in the passage suggest that Mickey is brave? Use information
from the passage to support your answer.

DIRECTIONS Be sure to:
- Write your answer in your own words.
- Write clearly.
- Check your answer after writing it.

_____

_____

_____

_____

_____

_____

_____

_____

Reading Comprehension

MSP Reading

Set 6

Instructions

Read each passage. Complete the exercise under each passage.

Then complete the questions on the next page. For each multiple-choice question, read the question carefully. Then select the best answer. Fill in the circle for the correct answer.

Thank You

Dear Grandma,

Thank you so much for the presents you sent me for my birthday! I am always amazed by how many wonderful things I receive. Of course, I had tried hard to be good all year. It is not easy to be good all the time, but I really tried hard. I have been polite and helpful to my friends and family.

This year, I got almost everything I asked for. This included a brand new bike. It is gold and sparkles like the Sun! I had wanted the puzzle you sent me for a long time as well. Thanks to you, I am going to try even harder to be good next year. I cannot wait for my birthday to come around again.

Lots of love,

Lucy

CORE SKILLS PRACTICE

This passage is a thank you letter. Write a letter to someone you know to thank them for something.

_____

_____

_____

_____

_____

_____

1 Read this sentence from the passage.

I have been polite and helpful to my friends and family.

Which word means the opposite of <u>polite</u>?

Ⓐ Mean

Ⓑ Kind

Ⓒ Giving

Ⓓ Rude

2 Which sentence from the passage contains a simile?

Ⓐ *Thank you so much for the presents you sent me for my birthday!*

Ⓑ *This year, I got almost everything I asked for.*

Ⓒ *It is gold and sparkles like the Sun!*

Ⓓ *I cannot wait for my birthday to come around again.*

3 Which statement would Lucy most likely agree with?

Ⓐ Making the effort to be good was worth it.

Ⓑ She should have been given more presents.

Ⓒ It is not important to be nice to others.

Ⓓ It feels good to give presents to others.

Something Special

Toby had played basketball for the school since he was eleven. When he reached sixteen, he was dropped from the team because his coach said he was too short. Toby was upset, but his father told him not to give up. He told him to keep playing and enjoying the game.

Toby played on the weekend with his friends. After school, he played by himself. Without anyone else to play with, he spent a lot of time learning ball skills. He enjoyed learning to do new things with the ball. But he missed playing in real games and being part of a team.

When they moved the following year, Toby trained with his new school team. His coach was impressed with his ball skills. Toby was delighted to be selected for the team. He later became the star player for his new team.

CORE SKILLS PRACTICE

This story is written from a third person point of view. This means it is written by someone who is not part of the story. Now imagine that the story is written from Toby's point of view. Write a paragraph from Toby's point of view describing being dropped from the team.

_____

_____

_____

_____

_____

_____

1   How does being dropped from the school team help Toby?

Ⓐ   He improves his ball skills.

Ⓑ   He decides to move.

Ⓒ   He gets other interests.

Ⓓ   He becomes upset.

2   What type of passage is "Something Special"?

Ⓐ   Realistic fiction

Ⓑ   Biography

Ⓒ   Science fiction

Ⓓ   Fable

3   What is Toby's main problem in the passage?

Ⓐ   He cannot play on the school basketball team.

Ⓑ   His friends are too busy to play with him.

Ⓒ   He is moving to a new school.

Ⓓ   He is chosen for a basketball team after he moves.

Brain Size

Did you know that the common ant has the largest brain in relation to its size? Of course, an ant's brain is much smaller than a human's brain. But the brain of an ant is 6 percent of its total body weight. The average human brain is just over 2 percent of a person's body weight.

A single ant brain has a fraction of the ability of a human one. But a colony of ants may have just as much ability. An average nest has 40,000 ants. In total, these ants would have about the same number of brain cells as a person.

CORE SKILLS PRACTICE

Describe three differences between the brain of an ant and the brain of a human.

1. _____

   _____

2. _____

   _____

3. _____

   _____

---

1   Where would this passage most likely be found?

    Ⓐ   In a science magazine

    Ⓑ   In a book of short stories

    Ⓒ   In an encyclopedia

    Ⓓ   In a travel guide

2   Why does the author begin the passage with a question?

    Ⓐ   To get readers interested in the topic of the passage

    Ⓑ   To show that the information may not be correct

    Ⓒ   To suggest that readers should research the topic

    Ⓓ   To indicate that there are facts to support the idea

3   According to the passage, how many ants are equal to one human brain?

    Ⓐ   2

    Ⓑ   6

    Ⓒ   20,000

    Ⓓ   40,000

Mosquitoes

It is well known that mosquitoes carry disease. But did you know that only females bite humans? Male mosquitoes only bite plants and greenery. Both genders carry over 100 separate diseases. It is the female of the species though, that passes these diseases onto members of the human race.

It was only in 1877 that British doctor Patrick Manson first discovered that mosquitoes could be very dangerous creatures.

CORE SKILLS PRACTICE

Sometimes you will be asked to make inferences. This means that you must guess something based on the information given. You can also sometimes use your own knowledge. Answer the question below by making an inference.

Why do you think mosquitoes are dangerous creatures?

_____

_____

_____

_____

_____

_____

---

1   Read this sentence from the passage.

Both genders carry over 100 separate diseases.

Which word means about the same as <u>separate</u>?

    Ⓐ   Different

    Ⓑ   Similar

    Ⓒ   Serious

    Ⓓ   Regular

2   Which detail explains why male mosquitoes do not pass on diseases?

    Ⓐ   Male mosquitoes do not carry diseases.

    Ⓑ   Male mosquitoes are not common.

    Ⓒ   Male mosquitoes do not bite people.

    Ⓓ   Male mosquitoes are unable to bite.

3   If the author added another sentence to the end of the passage, what would it most likely describe?

    Ⓐ   What Patrick Manson discovered about mosquitoes

    Ⓑ   How male and female mosquitoes are different

    Ⓒ   How to avoid being bitten by mosquitoes

    Ⓓ   Where mosquitoes can commonly be found

The Light

Christopher woke up late one evening. He was drawn to a light shining in through his window. He hurried downstairs and out into the back garden. Something bright and dazzling glimmered in the sky above him.

Christopher shielded his eyes as it moved towards him. It finally rested before him on the grass. As he stepped backwards, a door opened. A strange green outstretched arm welcomed him aboard. He paused, before stepping forward into the light.

CORE SKILLS PRACTICE

This story is about something strange that happens late at night. Think of something else strange that could happen late at night. Write your own short story describing a strange event.

_____

_____

_____

_____

_____

_____

_____

_____

1   Read this sentence from the passage.

He was drawn to a light shining in through his window.

What does the phrase "drawn to" mean in the sentence?

Ⓐ   Shocked by

Ⓑ   Woken up by

Ⓒ   Attracted to

Ⓓ   Sketched

2   What was Christopher most likely stepping onto?

Ⓐ   A car

Ⓑ   A bus

Ⓒ   A space ship

Ⓓ   A plane

3   What most likely caused Christopher to wake up?

Ⓐ   A loud noise

Ⓑ   A bright light

Ⓒ   A strange sight

Ⓓ   A bad dream

4   What do you think happens next in the passage? Use information from the passage to support your answer.

> **DIRECTIONS** Be sure to:
> - Write your answer in your own words.
> - Write clearly.
> - Check your answer after writing it.

_____

_____

_____

_____

_____

_____

_____

_____

Reading Comprehension

MSP Reading

Set 7

Instructions

Read each passage. Complete the exercise under each passage.

Then complete the questions on the next page. For each multiple-choice question, read the question carefully. Then select the best answer. Fill in the circle for the correct answer.

Peace and Not War

Terry was watching football in the lounge room, when his younger brother Mark walked in and changed the channel. Mark was determined to watch his favorite cartoon. They fought over the remote control. Then they started arguing.

"I hate watching football," Mark yelled.

"I hate watching cartoons," Terry yelled back.

Their voices got louder and louder. The lounge room began to sound like a zoo. Their mother came in from the kitchen. Without saying anything, she picked up the remote and turned off the television.

"If you can't watch the television nicely, then you can't watch it at all," she said.

CORE SKILLS PRACTICE

The author says that the lounge room began to sound like a zoo. What does the author mean by this?

_____

_____

_____

_____

_____

1   How is Mark different from Terry?

Ⓐ   He wants to watch television.

Ⓑ   He dislikes watching football.

Ⓒ   He yells louder.

Ⓓ   He dislikes cartoons.

2   Why did the mother most likely go into the lounge room?

Ⓐ   Because she had finished cooking

Ⓑ   Because she wanted to watch television

Ⓒ   Because she heard her sons fighting

Ⓓ   Because she wanted her sons to do their homework

3   What is the main lesson that the brothers learn in the passage?

Ⓐ   It is important to be quiet when inside.

Ⓑ   It is better to find a way to agree than to fight.

Ⓒ   Television is not important.

Ⓓ   There are too many programs on television.

The Dodo

The dodo was a species of flightless bird that became extinct. It lived on the island of Mauritius. It lived in an environment free from ground-based predators. When humans arrived on the island, they brought with them many ground-based animals. These included rats, pigs, and dogs. These animals ate dodo's eggs from their nests. The eggs were easy to get to because the nests were on the ground. Humans also hunted dodos for their meat. Humans also destroyed the dodo's forest habitats. The number of dodos decreased until they became extinct.

The dodo will always be remembered because it led to a common phrase. The slang phrase "as dead as a dodo" is used to describe something that is gone forever or definitely dead.

CORE SKILLS PRACTICE

Imagine you are asked to write a report on the dodo. Write a paragraph explaining why the dodo became extinct. You can use the information in the passage, but be sure to explain why the dodo became extinct in your own words.

_____

_____

_____

_____

_____

_____

1   Why did the author most likely include the second paragraph?

    Ⓐ   To tell an interesting detail about the dodo

    Ⓑ   To explain why dodos became extinct

    Ⓒ   To inform readers about how dodos lived

    Ⓓ   To suggest that the dodo should have been saved

2   Which of the following is NOT a reason that the dodo became extinct?

    Ⓐ   It was hunted for meat.

    Ⓑ   Its habitat was destroyed.

    Ⓒ   Its eggs were eaten by animals.

    Ⓓ   It caught human diseases.

3   How was the dodo different from most birds today?

    Ⓐ   It had wings.

    Ⓑ   It laid eggs.

    Ⓒ   Its nests were on the ground.

    Ⓓ   It had a number of predators.

Letter to the Editor

Dear Editor,

I am worried that our town park does not look as nice as it once did. It is not as well-cared for and is not cleaned as often. There are food wrappers, cans, and even broken glass lying around. I've noticed that there is a lot of graffiti appearing too.

I think that something must be done about this! It is no longer a lovely place to spend time. It is not even a safe place to play with all the trash lying around. The people of our town need to demand that something be done about this.

Yours with hope,

Evan

CORE SKILLS PRACTICE

This letter is written to complain about a town park not being clean. Write a short paragraph complaining about a problem in your city or town. In your paragraph, try to persuade the reader to take action to fix the problem.

_____

_____

_____

_____

_____

_____

1   The author says that the park is not a safe place to play. What item found in the park best supports this idea?

Ⓐ   Food wrappers

Ⓑ   Cans

Ⓒ   Broken glass

Ⓓ   Graffiti

2   What is the main purpose of the passage?

Ⓐ   To encourage people to visit the park

Ⓑ   To convince people that the park must be cleaned up

Ⓒ   To compare the park today with how the park was before

Ⓓ   To describe the different uses of the park

3   Read this sentence from the passage.

The people of our town need to demand that something be done about this.

Which word means about the same as demand?

Ⓐ   Offer

Ⓑ   Insist

Ⓒ   Plan

Ⓓ   Agree

Tom's Time Machine

Tom had spent almost a decade designing and building his time machine. He had spent countless hours in his laboratory. After he developed it, he had done many experiments sending small objects through time. And now, after all his hard work, it was finally time to test it for himself. He entered the time machine, and began to type into the computer.

Tom had always wanted to go back to the dinosaur age. He set the time to 80 million years ago. As the machine went dark and began to shake, he knew he was on his way deep into the unknown. He was scared, but thrilled with the idea that he might see a real dinosaur. He just hoped to himself that the first one he saw was a friendly one.

CORE SKILLS PRACTICE

Write a paragraph to add to the end of the story. In your paragraph, describe what happens when Tom sees his first dinosaur.

_____

_____

_____

_____

_____

_____

1   What does the illustration represent?

Ⓐ   How long it took Tom to create the time machine

Ⓑ   Where Tom plans to travel to in the time machine

Ⓒ   What the time machine looks like

Ⓓ   How the time machine works

2   What type of passage is "Tom's Time Machine"?

Ⓐ   Historical fiction

Ⓑ   Science fiction

Ⓒ   Autobiography

Ⓓ   Tall tale

3   Which word would Tom most likely use to describe his day?

Ⓐ   Frightening

Ⓑ   Exciting

Ⓒ   Boring

Ⓓ   Ordinary

Creature Comforts

Fred the farmer loved his job. He enjoyed nothing more than waking up at sunrise to feed and tend to his animals. He would even sing to them as he visited them in the morning. Even during the cold days of winter, he never once complained. He just put on thick socks and an extra coat and went out into the freezing cold air. The wind whipped around him and tried to annoy him. But Fred just focused on his tasks.

When the summer sun rose high in the sky and the day became very hot, he still loved working hard. He was always pleased knowing that he was making his animals happy and comfortable. Although they couldn't speak, Fred knew that his animals were happy with their life on his farm.

CORE SKILLS PRACTICE

Write a summary of what Fred's day is like.

_____

_____

_____

_____

_____

_____

_____

---

1   Read this sentence from the passage.

He enjoyed nothing more than waking up at sunrise to feed and tend to his animals.

What does the phrase "tend to" mean?

Ⓐ   Give water

Ⓑ   Sing to

Ⓒ   Look after

Ⓓ   Spend time with

2   What does the title of the passage suggest?

Ⓐ   That the animals on the farm are happy

Ⓑ   That Fred the farmer works too hard

Ⓒ   That many animals live on farms

Ⓓ   That animals make life easier

3   Which word best describes Fred?

Ⓐ   Kind

Ⓑ   Careless

Ⓒ   Impatient

Ⓓ   Amusing

4 Explain whether or not you think Fred is happy and content. Use information from the passage to support your answer.

DIRECTIONS Be sure to:
- Write your answer in your own words.
- Write clearly.
- Check your answer after writing it.

_____

_____

_____

_____

_____

_____

_____

_____

Reading Comprehension

MSP Reading

Set 8

Instructions

Read each passage. Complete the exercise under each passage.

Then complete the questions on the next page. For each multiple-choice question, read the question carefully. Then select the best answer. Fill in the circle for the correct answer.

Sugar

Did you know that sugar is a type of crystal? The crystal is edible. It is made out of a fructose molecule and a glucose molecule bonded together to form tiny crystals. It can form large crystals or fine crystals. Large crystals can be crushed or ground down to make finer crystals.

Under normal conditions, the molecules of sugar crystallize. When heated without water, the sugar crystals begin to melt. This process is called caramelization. This process is often used to make sweets such as toffees and syrups.

CORE SKILLS PRACTICE

Locate the information in the passage to answer the questions below.

What is a sugar crystal made of?

_____

_____

What is caramelization?

_____

_____

1   Read this sentence from the passage.

Large crystals can be crushed or ground down to make finer crystals.

What does the word <u>finer</u> mean as used in the sentence above?

Ⓐ   Nicer

Ⓑ   Sweeter

Ⓒ   Rounder

Ⓓ   Smaller

2   What would you be best to do if you wanted sugar to undergo caramelization?

Ⓐ   Place sugar crystals in boiling water

Ⓑ   Heat sugar crystals in a frying pan without water

Ⓒ   Crush sugar crystals into finer crystals

Ⓓ   Melt sugar crystals and then add some water

3   What is the main purpose of the passage?

Ⓐ   To instruct

Ⓑ   To entertain

Ⓒ   To persuade

Ⓓ   To inform

Herbal Tea

1. Add water to a kettle and wait until it has boiled.

2. Rinse the cup with boiling water to warm it up.

3. Place a tea bag and a teaspoon or two of sugar (if required) in the cup.

4. Add the water and allow to sit for 30 seconds.

5. Use a spoon to squeeze the tea bag. Then remove and stir the liquid.

6. Add a dash of milk or cream.

If you are making tea for several people, follow the same steps but use a teapot instead of a cup.

CORE SKILLS PRACTICE

The passage describes the steps of making tea in order. Think of a food or drink you know how to make. Write the steps for making that food or drink.

_____

_____

_____

_____

_____

_____

_____

1   Read this sentence from the passage.

Rinse the cup with boiling water to warm it up.

What is the meaning of the word <u>rinse</u> as used in the sentence above?

Ⓐ   Scrub

Ⓑ   Wash

Ⓒ   Soak

Ⓓ   Heat

2   What is the main purpose of the passage?

Ⓐ   To instruct

Ⓑ   To entertain

Ⓒ   To inform

Ⓓ   To persuade

3   Which step is carried out first when making tea?

Ⓐ   Adding sugar

Ⓑ   Adding milk or cream

Ⓒ   Squeezing the tea bag

Ⓓ   Rinsing the cup

A Day in the Life

Jenny was so proud of her father. He was a local police officer. Jenny's father took great pride in protecting people and keeping them safe. Jenny loved it when her father came home in the evening. He would talk about everything that happened that day.

Sometimes he would tell how he tracked down a thief. Other times, he would describe how he directed traffic after an accident. Another day, he might tell how he pulled over people who were speeding. Some days, all he did was sit at his desk and do paperwork.

No matter what he told her, Jenny was always impressed. When she slept at night, Jenny would dream that one day she would be like her father.

CORE SKILLS PRACTICE

The passage describes the day in the life of a police officer. Think of a different job. Describe the types of things someone with that job might do each day.

_____

_____

_____

_____

_____

_____

1   Read this sentence from the passage.

Jenny's father took great pride in protecting people and keeping them safe.

Which word or words best show what <u>protecting</u> means?

Ⓐ   *father*

Ⓑ   *great pride*

Ⓒ   *people*

Ⓓ   *keeping them safe*

2   What is the second paragraph mainly about?

Ⓐ   The tasks that Jenny's father does

Ⓑ   Why Jenny wants to be a police officer

Ⓒ   What Jenny thinks of her father

Ⓓ   The problems that police officer's have

3   Complete the web below using information from the passage.

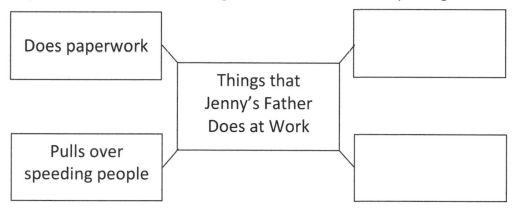

Silver

Silver is a shiny metal. It is the best conductor of both heat and electricity. Even though it conducts electricity well, silver is not often used in wiring. Copper is used in wiring because it is far cheaper to buy. Silver is also the most reflective of all the metals. It is used in mirrors and other reflective coatings. It is also used in photographic film. Another use is in solar panels and electronic devices such as mobile phones.

Silver is often used to make jewelry, cutlery, and items like serving plates. Silver can even be used to sterilize water. This has been known for a very long time. The Persian king Cyrus the Great had his water supply boiled and sealed in silver vessels.

Silver is also used to make coins and medals. Quarters, dimes, and nickels are not made from silver, but investors can buy coins made of silver.

Silver Use in 2011

Use of Silver	Percent Used
Photography	24%
Jewelry	20%
Silverware	12%
Coins and Medals	3%
Industrial Uses (such as solar panels and mobile phones)	40%

1   Read this sentence from the passage.

Copper is used in wiring because it is far cheaper to buy.

Which word means the opposite of <u>cheaper</u>?

Ⓐ   Easier

Ⓑ   Harder

Ⓒ   Dearer

Ⓓ   Duller

2   Based on the passage, why is silver rarely used in electrical wiring?

Ⓐ   It has too many other uses.

Ⓑ   It does not conduct electricity.

Ⓒ   It heats up too much.

Ⓓ   It is too expensive.

3   If the passage were given another title, which title would best fit?

Ⓐ   The History of Silver

Ⓑ   The Silver Spoon

Ⓒ   The Many Uses of Silver

Ⓓ   How to Spot Silver

Camels

Camels can survive for long periods of time without drinking water. The camel's hump is a big help with this. But it does not actually store water. It stores fat. The fat is used as a source of energy. Camels do store water. They store it in their bodies and in their blood.

Camels can go longer than 7 days without drinking. When they do find water, they can take a lot in. They are able to consume over 50 gallons of water at a time! These features allow them to survive in the desert.

Camels were once found in North America. They are now mainly found in the deserts of the African and Arabian regions.

CORE SKILLS PRACTICE

This passage has three paragraphs. Each paragraph has a different topic. Describe the topic of each paragraph. The topic of the first paragraph has been completed for you.

Paragraph 1: What the purpose of a camel's hump is

Paragraph 2: _____

Paragraph 3: _____

---

1 When a camel drinks 50 gallons of water, where would the water most likely be stored?

    Ⓐ   In its hump

    Ⓑ   In its stomach

    Ⓒ   In its blood

    Ⓓ   In its skin

2 What type of passage is "Camels" most like?

    Ⓐ   A short story

    Ⓑ   A news article

    Ⓒ   A magazine article

    Ⓓ   A fable

3 What is the main purpose of the passage?

    Ⓐ   To describe what a camel's hump is for

    Ⓑ   To explain how camels survive in deserts

    Ⓒ   To tell where camels are found

    Ⓓ   To show what camels look like

4   Explain how a camel's hump helps it survive without water. Use information from the passage to support your answer.

DIRECTIONS Be sure to:
- Write your answer in your own words.
- Write clearly.
- Check your answer after writing it.

_____

_____

_____

_____

_____

_____

_____

_____

Answer Key

Core Skills Practice

Each passage includes an exercise focused on one core skill described in the Common Core English Language Arts standards. The answer key identifies the core skill covered by each exercise, and describes what to look for in the student's response.

Reading Skills

The MSP Reading test given by the state of Washington tests a specific set of skills. The answer key identifies what skill each question is testing. Use the skill listed with each question to identify areas of weakness. Then target revision and instruction accordingly.

The answer key also includes notes on key reading skills that students will need to understand to master the MSP Reading test. Use the notes to review the questions with students so they gain a full understanding of these key reading skills.

Tracking Student Progress

Use the answer key to score the questions for each passage. After scoring the questions for each passage, record the score in the Score Tracker at the back of the book. Tally the scores to find the total once each set of 5 passages is complete.

As the student progresses through the sets, test scores will continue to improve as the students develops reading skills and gains confidence.

Set 1

The Basement Door

Core Skills Practice

Core skill: Write a narrative

Answer: The student should write a narrative about how Jake overcomes his fear of the basement.

Question	Answer	Reading Skill
1	C	Understand cause and effect
2	D	Identify the main idea
3	C	Use context to determine the meaning of words

The Rubik's Cube

Core Skills Practice

Core skill: Identify proper nouns

Answer: The student should list the proper nouns and their types below.

item	Rubik's Cube
nationality	Hungarian
person's name	Erno Rubik
company name	Ideal Toy Corp

Question	Answer	Reading Skill
1	A	Identify and use synonyms
2	D	Identify details that support a conclusion
3	C	Distinguish between fact and opinion*

*Key Reading Skill: Fact and Opinion

A fact is a statement that can be proven to be correct. An opinion is a statement that cannot be proven to be correct. An opinion is what somebody thinks about something. The sentence given in answer choice C is an opinion. It describes what the author thinks and cannot be proven to be true.

Learning Lines

Core Skills Practice

Core skill: Understand and analyze theme

Answer: The student should identify the theme as being about not giving up or the importance of hard work. The student should relate this theme to his or her own life.

Question	Answer	Reading Skill
1	C	Use context to determine the meaning of words
2	C	Make inferences about characters
3	A	Identify and summarize the theme of a passage

Sir Isaac Newton

Core Skills Practice

Core skill: Write an informative text

Answer: The student should list questions that would be appropriate to answer in a report.

Question	Answer	Reading Skill
1	C	Use words with multiple meanings*
2	C	Identify how a passage is organized
3	D	Locate facts and details in a passage

*Key Reading Skill: Multiple Meanings

Some words have more than one meaning. These words are known as homonyms. All the answer choices are possible meanings for the word *developed*. The correct answer is the one that states the meaning of the word *developed* as it is used in the sentence.

In the End

Core Skills Practice

Core skill: Compare and contract characters

Answer: The student should describe how Michael runs as fast as he can, while Stephen keeps a steady pace.

Question	Answer	Reading Skill
1	B	Use context to determine the meaning of words
2	A	Identify and summarize the theme of a passage
3	B	Identify how a passage is organized
4	See Below	Make inferences about characters

A complete answer should meet the criteria listed below. Give a score of 0, 1, 2, 3, or 4 based on how well the answer meets the criteria listed.

- It should make a valid inference about how Stephen feels after the race.
- It should include a fully-supported explanation of why the student believes this.
- It should use relevant details from the passage.
- It should be well-organized, clear, and easy to understand.

Set 2

Sarah's Diary

Core Skills Practice

Core skill: Form a personal opinion

Answer: The student should give an opinion on what benefits writing in a diary could have.

Question	Answer	Reading Skill
1	A	Use context to determine the meaning of words
2	D	Draw conclusions about characters
3	D	Identify point of view*

*Key Reading Skill: Point of View

The story is told by a person outside the story, so the passage has a third person point of view. There are two possible third person points of view. They are:

- Third person limited – the story is told by a person outside the story. The term *limited* refers to how much knowledge the narrator has. The narrator has knowledge of one character, but does not have knowledge beyond what that one character knows, sees, or does.
  Example: Jacky went for a hike in the mountains. After a while, her legs began to ache.
- Third person omniscient – the story is told by a person outside the story. The term *omniscient* refers to how much knowledge the narrator has. An omniscient narrator knows everything about all characters and has unlimited information.
  Example: Jacky went for a hike in the mountains. Like most of the other hikers, her legs began to ache.

The narrator is omniscient because he or she describes the thoughts and feelings of Sarah, Sarah's mother, and Sarah's sister.

Soccer

Core Skills Practice

Core skill: Summarize information in a passage

Answer: The student should complete the table with the details below.

        1. Brazil   5

        2. Italy   4

        3. Germany   3

Question	Answer	Reading Skill
1	A	Use words with multiple meanings*
2	D	Distinguish between fact and opinion*
3	A	Locate facts and details in a passage

*Key Reading Skill: Multiple Meanings

Some words have more than one meaning. These words are known as homonyms. All the answer choices are possible meanings for the word *object*. The correct answer is the one that states the meaning of the word *object* as it is used in the sentence.

*Key Reading Skill: Fact and Opinion

A fact is a statement that can be proven to be correct. An opinion is a statement that cannot be proven to be correct. An opinion is what somebody thinks about something. The sentence given in answer choice D is an opinion. It describes what the author thinks and cannot be proven to be true.

Pompeii

Core Skills Practice

Core skill: Determine word meanings

Answer: The student should write a valid definition of each word. Examples are given below.

partially: partly or only part of

destroyed: ruined

popular: liked by many people

Question	Answer	Reading Skill
1	B	Use prefixes and suffixes to determine the meaning of a word*
2	C	Identify the purpose of text features
3	A	Identify the author's main purpose

*Key Reading Skill: Prefixes and Suffixes

A prefix is a word part that is placed at the start of a word, such as *un-* or *dis-*. A suffix is a word part that is placed at the end of a word, such as *-less* or *-ly*. The word *rediscovered* is the base word *discovered* with the prefix *re-* added to the start. The meaning of *rediscovered* is "discovered again."

The Bumble Bee

Core Skills Practice

Core skill: Write a poem

Answer: The student should write a poem about an animal.

Question	Answer	Reading Skill
1	C	Locate facts and details in a passage
2	A	Understand and analyze literary techniques (alliteration)*
3	C	Identify the characteristics of poems

*Key Reading Skill: Alliteration

Alliteration is a literary technique where consonant sounds are repeated in neighboring words. The phrase "busily buzz" uses alliteration because of the repeated "b" sound.

Crying Wolf

Core Skills Practice

Core skill: Identify supporting details in a passage

Answer: The student should explain how the author shows that Jack is naughty. The student may describe how the author describes how Jack lies to his parents.

Question	Answer	Reading Skill
1	B	Make predictions about characters
2	C	Understand and analyze the plot of a passage
3	C	Identify and summarize the theme of a passage
4	See Below	Identify and summarize the theme of a passage

A complete answer should meet the criteria listed below. Give a score of 0, 1, 2, 3, or 4 based on how well the answer meets the criteria listed.

- It should identify the main message of the passage as being about always telling the truth, the consequences of lying, or being trusted by others.
- It should use relevant details from the passage.
- It should be well-organized, clear, and easy to understand.

Set 3

Big Ben

Core Skills Practice

Core skill: Locate facts and details in a passage

Answer: The student should answer the questions based on the information in the passage.
- Big Ben is in the United Kingdom.
- Big Ben is in the Palace of Westminster.
- Big Ben was built in 1858.
- Big Ben celebrated its 150th anniversary in 2009.

Question	Answer	Reading Skill
1	B	Identify and use antonyms*
2	A	Identify the author's main purpose
3	C	Distinguish between fact and opinion*

*Key Reading Skill: Antonyms

Antonyms are words that have opposite meanings. In this case, you are looking for the word that means "not pretty."

*Key Reading Skill: Fact and Opinion

A fact is a statement that can be proven to be correct. An opinion is a statement that cannot be proven to be correct. An opinion is what somebody thinks about something. The sentence given in answer choice C is an opinion. It describes what the author thinks and cannot be proven to be true.

Alexander Graham Bell

Core Skills Practice
Core skill: Make inferences
Answer: The student should make a valid inference about how Elisha Gray would have felt. The inference could be that Gray felt annoyed, angry, disappointed, or jealous.

Question	Answer	Reading Skill
1	D	Identify important and unimportant details
2	A	Identify different types of texts
3	B	Identify how a passage is organized

Penny the Princess

Core Skills Practice
Core skill: Understand cause and effect
Answer: The student should explain that meeting the homeless man makes Penny realize how lucky she is, or that it makes her decide to use her powers to help people.

Question	Answer	Reading Skill
1	D	Understand and analyze literary techniques (hyperbole)*
2	A	Understand and analyze the plot of a passage
3	D	Identify different types of texts

*Key Reading Skill: Hyperbole

The author uses hyperbole by stating that the castle "almost reached the clouds." The castle is described this way to emphasize its height.

Making Mistakes

Core Skills Practice
Core skill: Summarize a passage
Answer: The student should write a short summary of the story. The summary should include the main events from the story.

Question	Answer	Reading Skill
1	A	Identify and summarize the theme of a passage
2	D	Make inferences about characters
3	B	Draw conclusions about characters

Mount Mauna Kea

Core Skills Practice

Core skill: Understand visual information

Answer: The student should describe a diagram that shows the heights of Mount Everest and Mount Mauna Kea.

Question	Answer	Reading Skill
1	A	Identify and use antonyms*
2	D	Identify and summarize the main idea
3	B	Identify the main idea*
4	See Below	Compare and contrast two items

A complete answer should meet the criteria listed below. Give a score of 0, 1, 2, 3, or 4 based on how well the answer meets the criteria listed.

- It should identify how Mount Everest and Mount Mauna Kea are similar.
- It should identify how Mount Everest and Mount Mauna Kea are different.
- It should use relevant details from the passage.
- It should be well-organized, clear, and easy to understand.

*Key Reading Skill: Antonyms

Antonyms are words that have opposite meanings. In this case, you are looking for the word that means "not beneath."

*Key Reading Skill: Main Idea

One way that identifying the main idea is tested is by asking what would be another good title for the passage. The correct answer is a title that describes what the passage is mainly about.

Set 4

The First World War

Core Skills Practice

Core skill: Summarize a passage

Answer: The student should complete the table with the countries below.

The Central Powers: Austria, Hungary, Germany

The Allies: England, France, Russia, United States

Question	Answer	Reading Skill
1	B	Understand and analyze information shown on timelines
2	A	Identify different types of texts
3	D	Identify the author's main purpose

Football

Core Skills Practice

Core skill: Understand and interpret a passage

Answer: The student should give a title that relates to the topic or message of the passage, such as "A Surprising Choice" or "Girls Can Play Too!" The student should explain why the title suits the passage.

Question	Answer	Reading Skill
1	C	Identify the meaning of phrases
2	A	Draw conclusions based on information in a passage
3	B	Make inferences about characters

The Olympics

Core Skills Practice

Core skill: Write an opinion piece

Answer: The student should give an opinion on whether or not winning an Olympic medal is a worthwhile goal, and should support the opinion with a valid explanation.

Question	Answer	Reading Skill
1	A	Distinguish between fact and opinion*
2	B	Identify and use synonyms
3	D	Understand information in graphs, charts, or tables

*Key Reading Skill: Fact and Opinion

A fact is a statement that can be proven to be correct. An opinion is a statement that cannot be proven to be correct. An opinion is what somebody thinks about something. The sentence given in answer choice A is an opinion. It describes what the author thinks and cannot be proven to be true.

Air

Core Skills Practice

Core skill: Interpret visual information

Answer: The student should explain that the photograph helps show how nitrogen is added to the air by volcanoes.

Question	Answer	Reading Skill
1	C	Identify how a passage is organized
2	B	Locate facts and details in a passage
3	B	Analyze the use of features such as maps, graphs, and illustrations

The Waggiest Tail

Core Skills Practice

Core skill: Analyze an author's technique

Answer: The student may describe how the use of the words adds humor to the passage, or how it helps show how silly the argument is.

Question	Answer	Reading Skill
1	B	Identify and analyze different types of texts
2	C	Understand and analyze the plot of a passage
3	C	Locate facts and details in a passage
4	See Below	Identify and summarize the main idea of a passage

A complete answer should meet the criteria listed below. Give a score of 0, 1, 2, 3, or 4 based on how well the answer meets the criteria listed.

- It should identify the main idea of the passage as being about not arguing about silly things or about recognizing what is important.
- It should use relevant details from the passage.
- It should be well-organized, clear, and easy to understand.

Set 5

Beneath the Stars

Core Skills Practice

Core skill: Write an explanatory text

Answer: The student should write about something he or she enjoys doing. Students should describe what they like about it.

Question	Answer	Reading Skill
1	D	Understand and analyze word use
2	D	Make inferences about characters
3	D	Identify point of view*

*Key Reading Skill: Point of View

The story is told by a person outside the story, so the passage has a third person point of view. There are two possible third person points of view. They are:

- Third person limited – the story is told by a person outside the story. The term *limited* refers to how much knowledge the narrator has. The narrator has knowledge of one character, but does not have knowledge beyond what that one character knows, sees, or does.
  Example: Jacky went for a hike in the mountains. After a while, her legs began to ache.
- Third person omniscient – the story is told by a person outside the story. The term *omniscient* refers to how much knowledge the narrator has. An omniscient narrator knows everything about all characters and has unlimited information.
  Example: Jacky went for a hike in the mountains. Like most of the other hikers, her legs began to ache.

The narrator is omniscient because he or she describes the thoughts and feelings of Brian and Alice, including what Alice's dreams were like.

Dearest Donna

Core Skills Practice

Core skill: Identify audience and purpose

Answer: The student should identify that the audience is Donna, or may describe how the audience is the author's girlfriend. The student should explain that the poet wrote the poem to express his love.

Question	Answer	Reading Skill
1	D	Identify the tone of a passage*
2	D	Identify the characteristics of poems
3	C	Use context to determine the meaning of words

*Key Reading Skill: Tone

The tone of a passage refers to the author's attitude. It is how the author feels about the content of the passage. For example, the tone could be serious, sad, cheerful, or witty. In this case, the tone is loving.

Mozart

Core Skills Practice

Core skill: Summarize a passage

Answer: The student should write a short summary that includes the details below.
He worked as a court musician in Austria.
He looked for work and wrote music in Paris.
He wrote his best-known work in Vienna.

Question	Answer	Reading Skill
1	B	Use context to determine the meaning of words
2	B	Identify different types of texts
3	A	Identify the main idea*

*Key Reading Skill: Main Idea

One way that identifying the main idea is tested is by asking what would be another good title for the passage. The correct answer is a title that describes what the passage is mainly about.

Raindrops

Core Skills Practice

Core skill: Understand and use visual information

Answer: The student should complete the table. The middle column should show a raindrop shaped like a sphere. The far right column should show a raindrop shaped like a semicircle with the flat side on the bottom.

Question	Answer	Reading Skill
1	C	Use base words to determine the meaning of a word
2	B	Make predictions based on information in a passage
3	C	Identify the main idea

Visiting the Circus

Core Skills Practice

Core skill: Analyze a character in a story

Answer: The student may describe how Mickey feels nervous, how Mickey froze when the clowns came out, how Mickey told himself not to be afraid, or how Mickey's hands shook.

Question	Answer	Reading Skill
1	C	Use context to determine the meaning of words
2	A	Identify the main problem in a passage
3	B	Understand and analyze word use
4	See Below	Use details in a passage to support a conclusion

A complete answer should meet the criteria listed below. Give a score of 0, 1, 2, 3, or 4 based on how well the answer meets the criteria listed.

- It should provide a valid and well-supported argument about why Mickey can be considered brave.
- It should use relevant details from the passage.
- It should be well-organized, clear, and easy to understand.

Set 6

Thank You

Core Skills Practice
Core skill: Write a letter
Answer: The student should write a thank you letter to someone.

Question	Answer	Reading Skill
1	D	Identify and use antonyms*
2	C	Understand and analyze literary techniques (simile)*
3	A	Make inferences about characters

*Key Reading Skill: Antonyms

Antonyms are words that have opposite meanings. In this case, you are looking for the word that means "not polite."

*Key Reading Skill: Simile

A simile compares two things using the words "like" or "as." The phrase "sparkles like the Sun" is an example of a simile.

Something Special

Core Skills Practice
Core skill: Understand point of view
Answer: The student should write a paragraph describing Toby being dropped from the team. The narrative should be written in first person point of view.

Question	Answer	Reading Skill
1	A	Understand cause and effect
2	A	Identify different types of texts
3	A	Identify the main problem in a passage

Brain Size

Core Skills Practice

Core skill: Compare and contrast two items

Answer: The student should list the three differences below.

   1. The brain of an ant is smaller.

   2. The brain of an ant makes up a larger portion of its body weight.

   3. The brain of an ant has less ability.

Question	Answer	Reading Skill
1	A	Identify different types of texts
2	A	Identify the purpose of text features
3	D	Locate facts and details in a passage

Mosquitoes

Core Skills Practice

Core skill: Make inferences based on a passage

Answer: The student should make a valid inference about why mosquitoes are dangerous. The student should infer that mosquitoes pass diseases onto people.

Question	Answer	Reading Skill
1	A	Use context to determine the meaning of words
2	C	Draw conclusions based on information in a passage
3	A	Make predictions based on information in a passage

The Light

Core Skills Practice

Core skill: Write a narrative

Answer: The student should write a narrative about something strange happening late at night.

Question	Answer	Reading Skill
1	C	Identify the meaning of phrases
2	C	Make predictions based on information in a passage
3	B	Draw conclusions based on information in a passage
4	See Below	Make predictions based on information in a passage

A complete answer should meet the criteria listed below. Give a score of 0, 1, 2, 3, or 4 based on how well the answer meets the criteria listed.

- It should make a reasonable prediction about what happens next in the passage.
- The prediction made should be at least partly based on details given in the passage.
- It should use relevant details from the passage.
- It should be well-organized, clear, and easy to understand.

Set 7

Peace and Not War

Core Skills Practice

Core skill: Analyze an author's technique

Answer: The student should describe how saying the lounge room sounds like a zoo shows how noisy it was.

Question	Answer	Reading Skill
1	B	Compare and contrast characters
2	C	Make inferences about characters
3	B	Identify and summarize the theme of a passage

The Dodo

Core Skills Practice

Core skill: Write an explanatory text

Answer: The student should explain why the dodo became extinct. The reasons included may be that animals started eating the eggs, that people started hunting the dodos, and that the forests where the dodos lived started to be destroyed.

Question	Answer	Reading Skill
1	A	Identify the author's main purpose
2	D	Locate facts and details in a passage
3	C	Compare and contrast two items

Letter to the Editor

Core Skills Practice

Core skill: Write a persuasive text

Answer: The student should write a persuasive letter about solving a problem.

Question	Answer	Reading Skill
1	C	Identify details that support a conclusion
2	B	Identify the author's main purpose
3	B	Identify and use synonyms

Tom's Time Machine

Core Skills Practice
Core skill: Write a narrative
Answer: The student should write a paragraph that continues the story.

Question	Answer	Reading Skill
1	B	Understand and analyze illustrations and photographs
2	B	Identify different types of texts
3	B	Make inferences about characters

Creature Comforts

Core Skills Practice
Core skill: Summarize a passage
Answer: The student should write a short summary of what Fred's day is like based on the information in the passage.

Question	Answer	Reading Skill
1	C	Use context to determine the meaning of words
2	A	Draw conclusions about the features of passages
3	A	Draw conclusions about characters
4	See Below	Make inferences about characters

A complete answer should meet the criteria listed below. Give a score of 0, 1, 2, 3, or 4 based on how well the answer meets the criteria listed.

- It should state an opinion of whether or not Fred is happy and content.
- It should include a fully-supported explanation of why the student believes this.
- It should use relevant details from the passage.
- It should be well-organized, clear, and easy to understand.

Set 8

Sugar

Core Skills Practice

Core skill: Locate facts and details in a passage

Answer: The student should answer the questions based on the information in the passage.

     - A sugar crystal is made of a fructose and a glucose molecule.

     - Caramelization is the melting of the sugar crystals.

Question	Answer	Reading Skill
1	D	Use context to determine the meaning of words
2	B	Draw conclusions based on information in a passage
3	D	Identify the author's main purpose

Herbal Tea

Core Skills Practice

Core skill: Write an informative text

Answer: The student should describe the steps in making a food or drink.

Question	Answer	Reading Skill
1	B	Use context to determine the meaning of words
2	A	Identify the author's main purpose
3	D	Identify the sequence of events

A Day in the Life

Core Skills Practice

Core skill: Write an explanatory text

Answer: The student should describe what someone in a selected job would do each day.

Question	Answer	Reading Skill
1	D	Use context to determine the meaning of words
2	A	Identify the main idea
3	Tracks down thieves Directs traffic	Summarize information given in a passage

Silver

Question	Answer	Reading Skill
1	C	Identify and use antonyms*
2	D	Draw conclusions based on information in a passage
3	C	Identify the main idea*

*Key Reading Skill: Antonyms

Antonyms are words that have opposite meanings. In this case, you are looking for the word that means "not cheaper."

*Key Reading Skill: Main Idea

One way that identifying the main idea is tested is by asking what would be another good title for the passage. The correct answer is a title that describes what the passage is mainly about.

Camels

Core Skills Practice

Core skill: Identify main ideas

Answer: The student should identify the main topic of the second paragraph as being about how camels go without water, and the main topic of the third paragraph as being about where camels live.

Question	Answer	Reading Skill
1	C	Draw conclusions based on information in a passage
2	C	Identify different types of texts
3	B	Identify the author's main purpose
4	See Below	Summarize information given in a passage

A complete answer should meet the criteria listed below. Give a score of 0, 1, 2, 3, or 4 based on how well the answer meets the criteria listed.

- It should provide a correct and thorough explanation of how a camel's hump helps it survive without water.
- It should use relevant details from the passage.
- It should be well-organized, clear, and easy to understand.

Score Tracker

Set 1

The Basement Door	/3
The Rubik's Cube	/3
Learning Lines	/3
Sir Isaac Newton	/3
In the End	/7
Total	**/19**

Set 3

Big Ben	/3
Alexander Graham Bell	/3
Penny the Princess	/3
Making Mistakes	/3
Mount Mauna Kea	/7
Total	**/19**

Set 2

Sarah's Diary	/3
Soccer	/3
Pompeii	/3
The Bumble Bee	/3
Crying Wolf	/7
Total	**/19**

Set 4

The First World War	/3
Football	/3
The Olympics	/3
Air	/3
The Waggiest Tail	/7
Total	**/19**

Score Tracker

Set 5

Beneath the Stars	/3
Dearest Donna	/3
Mozart	/3
Raindrops	/3
Visiting the Circus	/7
Total	**/19**

Set 7

Peace and Not War	/3
The Dodo	/3
Letter to the Editor	/3
Tom's Time Machine	/3
Creature Comforts	/7
Total	**/19**

Set 6

Thank You	/3
Something Special	/3
Brain Size	/3
Mosquitoes	/3
The Light	/7
Total	**/19**

Set 8

Sugar	/3
Herbal Tea	/3
A Day in the Life	/3
Silver	/3
Camels	/7
Total	**/19**

Washington Test Prep Practice Test Book

Get a head start on the MSP Reading test taken by all grade 4 students! Get the Washington Test Prep Practice Test Book. It contains 8 reading mini-tests, focused vocabulary quizzes, plus a full-length MSP Reading practice test.

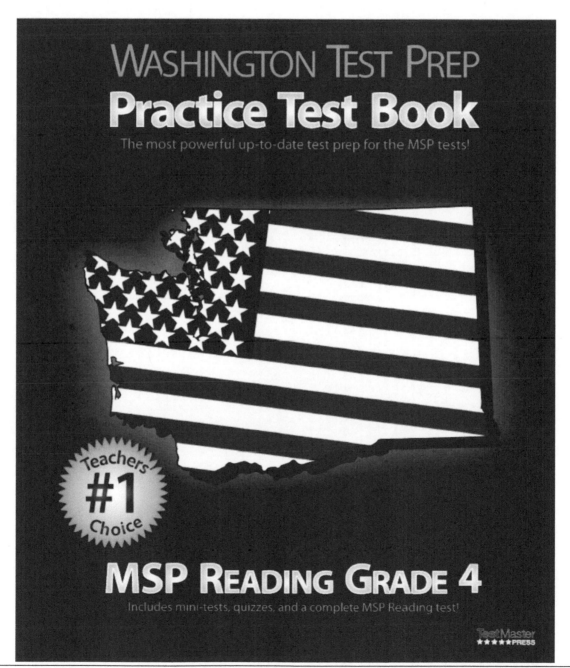